Vendors and Exhibitors Wanted!
Guide to Events

Julia A. Royston

BK Royston Publishing
P. O. Box 4321
Jeffersonville, IN 47131
http://www.bkroystonpublishing.com
bkroystonpublishing@gmail.com

© 2024

All Rights Reserved. No part of this book may be reproduced, stored in a retrieval system, or transmitted by any means without the written permission of the author.

Cover Design: Elite Cover Designs
Cover Photo: Licensed by AdobeStock 87721223

ISBN-13: 978-1-963136-40-1

Printed in the United States of America

Dedication

This is dedicated to anyone who ever thought about attending an event as a vendor or exhibitor no matter the industry or business.

Success. Lessons. Trials. Tribulations.

This is for you.

Acknowledgments

I thank my Lord and Savior Jesus Christ for giving me another opportunity to introduce more people to you. I thank you that you for entrusting this gift to me. Lord, let your Spirit move, guide and empower through this book and the people who will read it.

To my husband, Brian K. Royston for loving and cheering me on so much that I can be and do all that God has placed in me. I love you.

To my mom, my greatest supporter and best friend. To my Dad, who is in heaven, whom I know is proud of me and always encouraged me to go for it.

Thanks to all the rest of my family for their love and support.

A special thank you to Rev. and Mrs. Claude R. Royston for their love and support.

To the business owners who asked for this book, here it is. Go forth and prosper.

To the rest of my clients, social media friends and people that I've met along the way, thank you and love you always.

Let's go!

Love, Julia

#bookbusinessboss

Definitions

I may use the term vendor and exhibitor interchangeably, but I wanted to be clear from the start about the exact terms and definitions and what they mean technically. Now, how event hosts or promoters use a term is entirely left up to them. Don't get hung up on the terms, but be sure and read the requirements. Much more on this and other things in the upcoming chapters.

Event: something that happens or is regarded as happening; an occurrence, especially one of some importance.
The event can be inside a ballroom, convention center or church, outside under a tent or in the open air, or through virtual online streaming or pre-recorded. If it happened or is an occurrence, on a large or small, it's an event.

Exhibitor: a person or thing that exhibits. An exhibitor is primarily someone who shows their products or services and may or may not sell them at an event. I have been to events that labeled the venue "Exhibit Hall" or "Vendor Hall." Some participants sold product on the floor, and others just handed out information about their company or gave away brand promotional merchandise without selling it.

Vendor: a person or agency that sells. This definition is self-explanatory, but I have been to events where people displayed their products, but they weren't available for sale. You could order it, pay for it and they would ship to you later.

These are the three main definitions that I wanted to clarify upfront before we started. Because the costs to participate in events is going up every year, I want you to get the most from this book and apply the information to your business, product, service and life.

Let's go!

Table of Contents

Dedication	iii
Acknowledgements	v
Definitions	vii
Introduction	xi
Why Do Events Need Vendors or Exhibitors?	1
What's the Goal?	3
The Event	13
National and International Events	21
Regional and Local Events	39
Faith-Based Events	43
Coach/Speaker Platform Events	47
Non-Profit, Resource Events	51
Virtual Events	57
How Much Does It Cost?	61
Event Rules and Regulations	67
Communication	69
Event Promotion	73
The Offer	87
The Giveaway	93

The Vendor/Exhibitor Team	95
Event Checklist	103
Travel Tips	149
Things Not Mentioned in the Event Application, Description or Rules and Regulations	151
Unmet Expectations	
No Attendees	
No Inventory	
Terrible Placement on the Floor Plan	
Media Attention	161
Follow-Up	163
Don't Eat Up Your Seed	171
Let's Look at the Numbers	172
Next (Yes, No or One and Done)	179
Conclusion	187
About This Author	189
Other Books by This Author	191

Introduction

Welcome. I say "welcome" because I have been on a journey writing this book. I am about to take you on that same journey. I couldn't put everything in this book, but I tried to cover as many events, situations and possible solutions as I could. I am still on the journey and learning new things all of the time. Next, I will possibly use the terms "vendor" and "exhibitor" interchangeably, so don't be confused. I have given the definitions of each term early on so, hopefully, that will be settled in your mind, and the focus point will be on the information that I'm sharing.

The information is the star. Some of the information that I will share in this book is for large, national events, and other times you can use those same strategies even if you are alone at an event in a store or on the street with your products on display.

It doesn't matter just "go forth and prosper."

As much as I wanted to just focus on tips for being a vendor or exhibitor, I couldn't leave out the experiences I've had with preparing for, applying for, registering for, paying for and attending events. I couldn't leave out the different type of events that I have attended as well: Community Events, Church Events, Faith-Based National Events, Coach or Tribe Events, Non-Profit Events and Virtual Events. The event itself is the key to it all. It doesn't matter if the event is in a convention center, outdoor market or festival or a small round table in the inside of a store entryway; it's still an event and opportunity for you to represent your brand.

This book is all about learning, executing so that you can soar and grow in your business. Everybody starts where they start, regardless. Everyone has good days, bad days, great events and events that we wish we never attended. At the end of the day, I kept my word, pressed forward, promoted as hard as I could with the money I had and completed the assignment. That's all that you can do.

This book is birthed out of business owners' requests that represent various industries. This book is NOT JUST for authors, publishers or anyone in the literary industry. The strategies I include here can be applied to all industries.

I never intended to write this book but here we are. It was easy to write because I'm still living it. Entrepreneurship is not for the faint of heart, easily discouraged or for someone with very sensitive skin. You've got to toughen up, believe in yourself, believe in your products, services and if they don't want to buy it, move on to the next event with a new or different audience.

"Nothing ventured, nothing gained."

It's all a risk. For my brand, there are risks worth taking. I have something to offer that I am proud of. I'm not the BEST and not PERFECT but I have put my heart and soul into what I do and feel like I have something worth spending your money on for this generation and the ones to come.

Finally, as someone who has traveled and still travels the country putting more than 200,000 miles on the car, with the support of a great husband, Brian K. Royston, while sleeping in good and horrible hotel rooms, paying the vending prices and every other expense in between so that I can introduce, display and sell my products and services. I have sold my products from the back of my car, at a table or just the hallway of a ballroom, in the lobby of a church, outside under a tent in the rain, cold or heat, or freezing in an air-conditioned convention center, squeezed in a space that only can hold one round table and one chair, this is my story and I'll do it again until it's time to stop. This book is my perspective and lessons that I have learned along the way.

As the young people say today, "no shade," no critique, just a girl sharing her journey.

Let's go!

Why Do Events Need Vendors or Exhibitors?

Let's be honest: some event organizers don't always have vendors or exhibitors at their events. You come in, register, get your information and enjoy the conference, workshop and/or event. It is not required to have vendors or exhibitors at events. That's the disclaimer for the "why" of vendors and exhibitors. But the #1 reason is money, income, profit and — hopefully — additional help with promotion for the event. The vendors pay up front. Even if ticket sales are low, hopefully, the event host is smart enough to have enough vendors to pay for the venue space because it is so expensive.

Now, some events don't have vendors but the ticket price is at a level to cover the venue costs, any food fees, other amenities and if done right, will still make a nice profit.

Every promoter/host doesn't do this, but my hope is always that they spotlight, highlight and allow time for people to visit and support the vendors who really helped sponsor the event. The majority of the time, the host/promoter has made their money up front.

I have gone to events where the vendors have been ignored, overlooked, never mentioned and not thanked for being at the event, but know this: I probably didn't return to that event another year and pay that organization any more vendor fees.

For the purpose of this book, I want to point out things for business owners to be looking for to make the most out of paying to attend events. For those who want to host events, this book will help you get the perspective of the vendor/exhibitor. My friends call me "the Queen of Events" because I attend so many events. I also share event ads for my clients to attend events and represent clients who aren't able or desire to attend events. My experience is attending local, regional and national events.

Take notes on what applies to you or what you may have questions about and if you need my help, visit www.talkwithroyston.com to schedule a conversation. Let's go!

What's the Goal

The Goal

I have taken this on as a mantra for myself, my business and my life, but I must give credit to whom credit is due. My friend, Vanessa Collins says before we start any project, ask what's the goal and the offer? We must start with the end "game" or end "goal" in mind. Where are we trying to do with the product, service or business? What are the steps that we are taking to get there? How will we know when we have accomplished or missed our goal? What is the test that will determine if we should or should not attend this event ever again?

I know what will determine the answers for me and my business but let's help you answer some of these questions for you and your business.

Sales, Profit

Whether you have a for-profit business or a non-profit business, you have to have profit, sales, income, grant, donations or an endowment to generate revenue to stay in business. I don't care what type of business it is or what industry that it represents, you must have money and profits to stay in business. That is normally the #1 goal for any business owner attending an event and that is sales.

What is the #1 way to make sales at an event? Show up. Show up with inventory. Show up on time. I can't tell you how many places I have been where the people don't show up on time or not at all. I'll get into more details later but for now just remember to show up on time. Income makes the business go and grow. The Bible says, "Money answers all things," which is true. But money managed, invested and generated can not only answer, but can also demand and get some things, too. Sales, profit and income is the #1 goal but what if something happens and no one shows up? Is that the only reason, goal and test of the success or failure of attending an event?

Let's explore more.

Introduction

Some events are designed to introduce you to a new audience. These people are just meeting you; do you expect them to buy from you on the first meeting? Of course, you do, but people don't always buy on the first encounter. Have you ever gone to a job interview and you're meeting the interviewer for the first time? Of course, we all have. You invested money, time, your best suit/outfit, got your hair and nails done and the shoes were on point too. Did you get the job? Sometimes yes and sometimes no. Why? They are just meeting you and comparing you with the other applicants. The same applies to being at events, especially large events. If there are thousands of people, there also may be hundreds of vendors. The people have choices, they may have a limited budget and based on your approach, products, smile, interest, body language and pricing, it can determine the results. I have stories for days and will also share pictures of the many events that I attended over the years. Some of the events, I sold nothing! Why? It was an introduction. The people may have liked what I was selling or liked me but they didn't want what I had to offer enough to pay for it. It's a harsh reality but one you must be ready for. It's hard to understand, explain and comprehend but true. It's even harder to explain to family members who have seen your level of investment but the return on that investment is slow and small. I can't tell you how many years I didn't turn a profit on the things, places and people I invested in, but I kept going.

Short story; I attended an event and it was NOT profitable. But with the visibility at that event, I was able to profit later from meeting the people at that event. Show up. Be prepared. Don't stop. Keep going. We'll explain further what to do at an introduction event later.

Networking

If you are a natural introvert, networking is hard. Who enjoys going into a room knowing no one but having to act enthusiastic? You don't know whether to just smile, try to give them a card, shake their hand, nod your head or just fist bump them. You don't know these people! You didn't really want to come but thought you would meet someone new, possibly sell something but realize that it was more of a networking event rather than a sales event. At some events, you are able to "showcase" what you have to offer, sell it and profit from it. At some events, selling is NOT allowed on the floor or during the event. Ouch! I went to one of those events and paid money to be there! Why? So, I can tell you how to handle yourself, position your business and profit from the event even if you can't sell on the tradeshow floor. More to come.

Positioning

My definition of "positioning" is getting in front of, in close proximity to and with the opportunity to pitch to people or organizations that could want or need what I have to offer. I purchase a vendor/exhibitor booth to position myself, business and products in the best light and in front of a targeted audience for a chance of a 'yes.' I think that maybe a new book title for me. How much are you willing to invest for a chance at a yes? That's what positioning does, hopefully: it puts you in the best position for that "yes."

I'm a risk taker and willing to risk money, effort and time for the "yes." Being in business is a risk. You have to take a risk. Being at events is a risk. There are no guarantees. Before you sign up, fill out the application or submit the fee, you have to okay with taking a chance for a "yes."

Potential Partnerships

We can't partner with everybody. That's just the way life is. People's behavior, investment plus results do not always guarantee success.

So why should you partner? First off, connect with the person on a personal level. Can you work with them, and can they work with you? Secondly, although you can do it alone, it can be better when you're working with someone else on the project or event. It should lessen the load. Hopefully, they have ideas that are different from yours and sometimes, even better ideas that can make the project an even greater success. Thirdly, even if you do the same thing or in the same type of industry, you may approach the work differently. If you're open to it, can be a good thing. Next, there may be other services, information and tools that you need to be better. Partnering with someone who does that well instead of having to learn something brand new makes tasks move quicker. For example, I have friends who are experts in digital marketing, creating videos and influencing. Instead of trying to do that myself, I have them on my platform to partner and teach my clients and I learn as well. I have a good friend LaShaunda Hoffman who is the Queen of Book Promotion. I promote books as well, but when I need to know what's trending that works well, why not call on, get trained by or have as a guest someone who specializes in it to partner with instead of running myself ragged to learn something new when my sister from Missouri already does it. Can you think of anyone right now whom you could or should be partnering with? Not yet? I'll keep going.

There are times when you do find people that you can partner with at events. I had three booths at the Indiana Black Expo and there were several authors and publisher that were there. One publisher in particular, Denola Burton, talked to me. We connected and we have been on several events together and will probably do more things together if our schedules permit. She has two thriving businesses and I have several as well, but when our schedules coincide, we make it work. That's partnership. There are other people whom you meet who are divine connections and once you meet them, connect, collaborate and partner with them, you are partners for life. This is very rare and if you find it, hold on to that partnership and relationship for life. That is my friend, Vanessa Collins. We met at her church. I was singing. She and her family were relocating 10 minutes from me. We have been neighbors now for 15+ years. Partnered in several events, online and in-person and will support each other for life.

What happens when partnerships evolve, change or the other expands or grows? Remember that people change, goals change, and life creates change so be ready for that. Second, if things are not changing in some areas of your life and business, you may be stagnant, in a rut and not growing. Therefore, prepare for, be ready for, know going in and allow partnerships to evolve and change. If the partnership works go back to your why and always remember why you partnered up in the first place. Know that relationships are gold and currency that can't be replaced easily. Say sorry. Apologize. Air out any differences but don't let it separate you from the real reason you partnered.

I lingered on this topic because it is so rare to find people who will partner with you and stay friends even if the partnership changes, evolves or dissolves. Find your partner, tribe and community. When there is understanding, commitment and respect, it is a win/win on so many levels. Partner with a purpose.

Expansion

When I am at events, I am also wanting to learn as much as I can. I've been in business for 16+ years and know a lot, but I don't know everything. I am still learning, growing, experimenting and striving to be better each and every year. I attended an international trade show and knew that I was the little man in the room. I gave it my all and my best to compete, but I knew I had stepped into the big leagues. It was an opportunity for me to expand, grow, see and learn. That trade show was a college education administered in one week. Now, I handled my business, made some connections, sold some product and took some notes but knew that when I got home, I had some decisions to make. If I attend more of this level event, I need grow more, save my money and next time, be bigger and better than ever. I now take pictures of other people's trade show displays, store them on my server so that I can grow to that level on my next presentation.

There should be some events that you go to that you come away feeling inadequate and know that there is room to grow. Be able to take time to walk the floor layout so that you can learn and expand for the next time. You have paid to be there and once you're there, get an education on the money that you've spent. Don't let your time there be just for present event but invest in your future.

Ask yourself first, what's the goal?

The Event

Before we can set up, buy inventory or check anything else on the checklist, we have to get the details about the event.

Do your homework and get these questions answered.

What is the name of the event?

The title will give you some information right there if it is listed as a Festival, Workshop, Summit or Convention. I had one event host state in the interest email that the event was not a normal festival and expenses to attend should be considered prior to registering. Well, that turned me off right there. Why? You're trying to give me a disclaimer that the event is not well attended and worth it for people who have to come far or outside the state limits. It wasn't a small hint but a huge cue for me and I didn't register.

Where is it being held?

Is the event at a convention center with a loading dock and easy access to the ballroom?

Is the event at a church, school, hotel or other venue? This will determine difficulty or ease of access into the building. Also, are there steps, is there an elevator or will we have to carry the boxes and inventory up steps. I went to an event and they failed to mention that the access was via steps and limited elevator space. I went one more time with very little inventory because I remembered the steps. I didn't attend again. I had two reasons. It was inconvenient and not well attended.

Outside vs. Inside Event

I prefer inside events. I have done outside events in the past, but I am really not a fan of outside events with portable toilets, I am getting older, and outside is not my first choice. I like inside events with cushy chairs, good signage and good promotion. There are events that I do attend that are outside, but it is because it is well attended, I make great sales and connections. It may sound petty, but if I am going to be at an event for three days for 10 hours a day, the amenities are important to me. (LOL) Once, I attended to an event and they ran out of space in the main ballroom. They offered me a table outside of the room and I said "yes." "Why" you ask? Well, firstly, it was crowded in the main room and I am not a little lady. With all of the traffic in the hotel, I found out that there were two other events there at the same time. Three events, three times the audience and only 1 vending fee. It was great.

When is it being held?

Be aware of the events held during a holiday. I'm not talking about Christmas and/or the shopping holidays but Mother's Day, Father's Day, Easter, etc. Mother's Day is such a family weekend, so I am always very careful about attending or vending at these events unless it is an event that they've been hosting for years, sponsored by an organization with a great reputation and well attended. In Louisville, Kentucky, the first Saturday in May is the Kentucky Derby, but one of the sororities has a huge brunch held on that day attended by well over 2,000 women. They come ready to buy even though the tickets are $50+ each. Although it is a Louisville holiday, I normally don't miss that brunch because it is well attended every single year.

Juneteenth is a holiday in June that has great prominence with the African American community. The activities spotlight Black owned-businesses, and most of the larger cities have very well-attended events. Some holidays are great for participation and should be considered wisely if the past events have been successful.

Who is the host of the event?

Now, I realize that this shouldn't matter, but it does. You need to know who, their history, their business and their reputation. Why? Because the primary audience is normally connected to, attracted to, follows, sees the ads on social media, is on the email list, has registered in the coaching program and attends the same church, meetings and events of the host. Knowing your product, service and audience vs. the host's product, service and audience will make a difference as to whether you attend or not. Has the host been promoting the event for quite some time? Does the host have experience in hosting events small or large? There should be some social media or website evidence or "receipts" (as the young people say) to prove it. What have been the reviews or results from people attending the event? As the potential vendor, do you have similar or different products and services as the host? As a business owner, you attract people for not only what you do but who you are. Do your homework. Success leaves clues. Once you've done your homework, you should be able to make a decision as to whether you want to participate or not. Let's go!

Who is their target audience for the event?

We are going to talk about a prospectus later but at a minimum, the event host should provide information on target audience for the event. As a book publisher, I have invested highly in children's books, so I am looking for attendees that either have children, serve families with children or educators, etc., especially children of color. I have attended events with multicultural attendees and have had people of all races purchase my books. Having a target audience is important but don't be limited as to whom is eligible to purchase whatever you have to offer. You will be surprised who will be attracted to what you have to offer even if they are not your initial or profiled target audience. As stated in chapter one, what is your goal, target or intended result? You should start with the end in mind, but if you are fortunate enough to gain other clients and those interested along the way, more power to you.

What is the Event Goal and Mission?

I know that the flyer, Eventbrite page, landing page or full website will give some information, but with Artificial Intelligence (AI), the event can sound wonderful but, what is the event's real goal and mission?

Check out these following key things to consider before paying your hard-earned money for a vendor table or booth:

- Is there an email address available to ask for more information?
- Is there a website with a recap video or images from the previous year's event even if it is just a post on Facebook.
- How long have they been hosting this event?

- What is the expected attendance to the event?
- If it is an outside event, will it go on whether rain or shine, or could it be cancelled? If cancelled, is there a refund policy or no refund?

I'm sorry to say, but even if the event has been going on for years, it still doesn't mean that the event is successful for the vendors. Some hosts — not all — but some hosts get the vending fee and make lots of money, but in actuality, the host is the only one benefiting from the event. The vendors have paid for everything, but the real beneficiary is the host.

Has anyone you know ever been to the events? If not, post on social media about the event and review responses.

Social media is a wonderful way to find out people's opinions. You can ask people to inbox (or "DM" for direct message) you if they don't want their comment public. Be careful, consider their advice and then make your own decision. There have been times that no one responded. I reach out to people that I know in that area of the event to help me make my decision. Once I decide, I don't look back. Some events may be only for you, your business and products and not someone else's. Always make the decision that is best for you, your products and your brand. If it is a success or failure, it was based on your research, results and decision.

National and International Events

A Prospectus

National and international trade shows normally, provide a prospectus or what I call a report of their event. Like a business annual report, they can tell you the people that attends their event, how many people and attended in the past, the industry, their career positions and other demographics. The prospectus usually gives a history of the event, if it is an annual event and sometimes, their future events. The prospectus tells you vendor/exhibitor hall layout, the fees, what the fees include, set-up times, break-down times, the event schedule, the rules and logistics of the event. Events that provide a prospectus normally have a separate shipping, set-up and management company for the event. These companies will be the contact while you are at the event for anything on the show floor, trash, storage, moving in and out, delivery of your products, electricity, carpet, chairs, table and anything else you need at the tradeshow. They charge fees for these services.

These companies are contracted by the hosting company to provide all logistic services for the exhibitors before, during and after the event.

They have been specifically contracted so that the event/host/promotional organization can focus on driving the traffic to the event, the workshops/speakers and other marketing and promotional efforts. These events normally are held in large convention centers or hotels that can accommodate a large event. These events have vending fees of $1,000+ and do not provide refunds and each service that you request is a fee. Read, read and re-read the prospectus. Know exactly who is going to attend, what the fee is and what that fee includes, what the schedule and length of the conference is, location of the conference in the city, location of the conference in the convention center, location of the vendors in relation to where the flow of traffic and other activities are going to be held. When can you check-in? Will vending services be on site to answer questions and help you solve any issues that you have? Read all of this, email the contact with any questions and be clear of the answers to your questions, BEFORE you pay the vending fee. With larger events, the fees are in the thousands and often require weeks before you can think about getting a refund. Do your homework.

Event Schedule

Early on with attending events, I just assumed so much. Not anymore. The dates of the event on the promotional flyer do not necessarily determine when the attendees will be there and have access to the exhibit hall versus when the leadership team will be meeting, pre-conference workshops, etc. If the flyer states that the event is from March 1–5 of whatever year, make sure to know exactly when the vendor/exhibit space opens, when you can move in and when the exhibitor space/room/hall will be open. Oftentimes, the beginning of the event is only for the leadership and special sessions, but the vendor hall is not open until 1–2 days later. For example, March 1–2 may be for the leaders only, and the exhibit hall doesn't open until March 3–5. The vending fee for the event doesn't change but depending on when you actually need to be there to move-in, etc. your expenses for your travel, etc. may change. Be sure that you know exactly how many hours on the schedule will be dedicated to the exhibitor halls and for attendees to have access and support your business.

Additional questions to ask are:

- Is there time throughout the event to visit vendors?
- Are the vendors acknowledged or spotlighted in a program or video presentation, even if it is a paid spotlight.? (Note: you may have to pay extra for this spotlight.
- What is the proximity to the main event room?
- Are the exhibitors in the same room, next door, down the hall or on a different floor?

I have also seen prospectuses where the vendors were also located across the street in another building. There were workshops in that same building, but only temporarily, so the traffic for the majority of the audience would not be coming to that building or be supporting your business.

Traffic Flow

Based on the schedule and the layout of the conference in the prospectus, how are people coming to the vendor/exhibitor area? "Believe you me," there is an agenda, a flow and a purpose behind everything at this type of event. There is usually a method to get the people inside the building from the parking lot, street or other entrances, moving in and out from workshop room to room and then back to the main hall and then past the exhibit hall, from sessions to session and even the location of the bathrooms, food, parking, etc., has been considered. As a vendor, you are helping to pay for this event. Ask all of the questions that you want.

Booth Selection

Most, not all but most, larger, higher-priced vending events allow you to select your booth location. Why? At the price point that they set, you should be able to select the booth and not have to walk up and down the aisles to find out where your booth is with all of your heavy carts, boxes, etc.

If you get to select your booth space, make sure that you register early as possible and get the best access possible. Booth space selection is on a first come, first serve basis.

Knowing the booth space up front, also allows time, direction and location for better promotion. Your current or future clients want to find you easily so make sure that you tell them your booth/space number. They may or may not find you, and thus, you lose out on a client or sale.

What's my preferred spot at a trade show? On a corner, near the food, near the bathroom or at an entrance. Why? #1, a corner booth allows you to have more than one table in the booth. This gives you the ability to display and sell more product. If possible, I take the side railing and draping off of the side that opens onto an aisle way. Don't do this if it will damage the booth behind you in any way, but take off most of the side railing so that people can walk right up to the booth table even closer and see what you have to offer.

In the image below, I actually have three tables in the booth.

Additionally, because I have a corner, we can monitor the traffic going two directions. As you can see how my husband is positioned in the image above, he takes the aisle and I take the front. We are able to connect with the audience in two directions. If you look closely at the bottom of the table, you will see the carpet that we had to buy for this show. Hint: Read the prospectus carefully.

Also, some large trade shows have you listed at a particular booth space on the show floor layout on the website, digital and printed programs. This is additional marketing and promotional opportunities for you and your business. This provides proof of your past shows and gives you credibility for future shows.

There are also table events that do not have drapes, dividers, etc. but it is an open area/table event. See image below:

If this had been a local event, I probably could have fit another table behind or adjacent to the main table and still not blocked anyone else's table. Additionally, it would have allowed for more product on the table, which in turn would have the opportunity for more profits.

The next image is another corner table setup, which allowed for a lot more space for people to access our product. There were only four booths connected, so you can imagine the wide walkways, increased traffic pattern and space of product.

Now this image shows my favorite spot at a trade show and that is in a front entrance to the exhibit hall. You can see the traffic at this event as well. I've been going for at least 8-10 years and will continue do the traffic, sales and connections.

The image below is another table entrance access point. I don't like having my back to the door but when people entered, they look left and right. They also circle the entire room and look at every table which is wonderful.

Being at an entrance doesn't guarantee you sales but it gives you a great head start.

Okay, I love being at a corner, but there are times it doesn't work out like that and your books are hidden behind or beside clothes. Be sure to speak to everyone who comes by to see the clothing booth. Why? They may stop by your booth on the way to the clothing. Make friends with the vendors nearby and make sure to do your best to be seen and heard. It may look like a loss but let the clothes bring the potential customers to you. I have had vendors with product totally different than mine recommend me to their customers as well. It was a win all of the way around.

Accepted or Rejected

Amazingly enough, there are some shows that require that you apply to be a part of their show and they determine whether they accept you or not. Even if you have the money to pay, they can deny you access to their audience. I know that is hard to believe but it happens. There can be many reasons or criteria to accept or reject businesses.

One reason is that you have been to an 'equal sized or level show' as the show that you are applying for admission to. What I mean by "equal level show" is that the previous show or event that you attended can mirror the applied show in location, size, target audience and show objectives/results. Most industries have key players that know each other. Most large trade shows have the same representative/moving companies, and they understand the assignment and the level and reputation of the companies that participate in these shows. So, if a show requires that you tell your past attendance, they will know and then decide on your participation or not.

I realize that some of you are only thinking about the large shows in the convention centers, expo centers, etc., but don't be surprised at the small, local, community events that have the same big event mentality and will vet/research you just as hard. I'm from Kentucky, born and raised, and an event in Kentucky denied me access because I didn't have enough Instagram followers and you live 75 miles away, it hurt and I haven't forgotten it.

On the hand, I've been at events where the people knew how much you paid to be there, and they wanted to take my picture because of the sacrifice. It's amazing. Remember this book is let you in on my experiences, better understand this part of business and help you on your quest for getting your products in front of new audiences to be profitable.

Get References

Contact other companies who have been at the event that are in your same industry. Quick sidebar and hint: Be able to compete in your same industry but also build relationships so you can trust someone to communicate, collaborate, network and learn from. You won't make it in business if you remain on an island to yourself. Everyone is not your enemy.

There is someone who is willing to listen, empathize or sympathize even if they don't fully understand your business and industry. If they are retired or no longer in business, at least they will understand what you're going through.

It will save you time, effort and money if you ask someone up front about the event. Now there will be people who may lie and not tell the truth, but at least you did your homework.

Typical questions ask are: how was the venue, how was the set-up, did you pick your own space or were the spaces/booths assigned, was the event well attended, did the attendees support/buy or just walk through, look and didn't buy anything. Were the vendors spotlighted in any way, was there ample enough time in the schedule for people to visit the vendors and what were the results?

Be mindful of the business products that the referenced business is selling. You results may not be equal if for example, you sell books and they sell clothing or purses. The results will be vastly different. If you sell clothes, talk to someone who also sells clothes. You get the idea. As a vendor or exhibitor, keep in mind the seasons of the year, what is also going on in the city as well as the location of the event. Rain, snow or bad weather with an outside event won't do well, but if it is a pretty day, inside, comfortable, well promoted, make sure you have plenty of product.

In conclusion, ask questions, get references so that you make an educated, knowledgeable decision before spending your money on the vending fee or inventory.

Notes

Regional and Local Events

Regional

Most of the same things that I said with regards to local events applies to regional events, but the audience is larger and has greater potential to reach more people. Now, I was born in Kentucky, live in Indiana and Ohio is just down the street 100 miles away. So, I live and have access to the great tri-state area of Indiana, Kentucky and Ohio. With 3 states so close, I can attend multiple events, build a larger community, have access to a wider network and can potentially make money at three times the rate by staying connected to events and people on a regional basis. For example, in September of 2023, I had a team at an event in Louisville, Kentucky, I was in Indianapolis, Indiana, at another event, and if I needed somebody else to be in Cincinnati, Ohio, I could have as well because it is a close travel distance. Be able to have regional access alone could be a reason for a building a vending/sales team.

I mentioned the larger, national/international events first because they have requirements of more budget, time and audience. I highly suggest that you start off with local events, then move to regional events and then tackle a national/international event. It gives you experience, preparation and information that you will need with the larger trade show/national/international events.

Local Event

To start with, for most local events in your area, you will either know the person hosting the event or can find out easily. There are some events in your area that may be hosted by someone from out of town but if the person hosting is local, you can find people online or in your circle of connections who has attended the event and share their results. As forementioned, make sure that the person you are asking has products/services that are similar to yours and if their products/services are NOT similar, take that into strong consideration.

Because the event is local, there should be minimal travel expenses, such as gas, parking and the vendor fee. There should be no hotel expenses unless you just want to stay at the host hotel for convenience. I was recently in Atlanta and the staff members stayed in the host hotel because it was connected to the convention center, and if you know Atlanta traffic, you see why. Also, the parking lot charged coming in and going out, so there were no "in and out" privileges so that matters, too. But I love local events because I get to sleep at home in my own bed. LOL Now being local can be a win and lose situation. The downside of being at a local event is that some people feel like they can see you and purchase from you anytime because you are local. Because I travel on a regular basis, people know that they don't see me all of the time and they will support if they want what I have to offer. I'm not all over town, all of the time. On the other hand, it is a win because I can literally draw, notify and help promote people to the event better because I am right there in the same city.

As a vendor at a local event, you are also keeping and moving money in the community, which is always helpful to the local economy, attention to the community, good for networking and collaboration.

Notes

Faith-Based Events

I mentioned earlier about these hosted events so now I want to address it. First, let me offer a disclaimer that I am a faith-based person, so this is nothing against faith-based events. Secondly, I have been at a faith-based event as a speaker and as a vendor. Finally, this section is for those who want to embark as a speaker and/or a vendor at one of these events. So let me explain exactly what I mean.

The faith-based national/regional/local events draw people, which is great. I have been blessed, supported and presented at faith-based events on all levels. But all faith-based events are not alike. The support will depend on the objective of the event, the audience, the time or season of the month in which the event is held and the access to the audience and their particular budget. You can't control any of these aforementioned things. They are solely left up to the host, but you should be aware of these things so that you can make an honest, informed and educated decision about your participation.

For the larger denominational faith-based conferences, they are used to coming to the vendor area, spending their money and supporting. It is a part of the nature and history of the event and the culture of the people. It is what they do. The main thing that will stop them is if you don't have what they want, or the price point is too high for what you're offering. They can want it but if they don't have the budget set aside for it, they won't buy it. On the other hand, some people come to the vending area to shop specifically because they are not able to obtain the products and/or services in their local or regional area. They know at the national event, what they want will be there and they bring the money to pay for it. On the other hand, there are some faith-based events that the audience wants what you have but they have spent their money inside of the conference during the offertory, at the registration desk or just don't have the money to spend because of travel and accommodations. It is based on the economy, the product and/or service that you are offering. Remember I sell books for children, adults, business, inspirational and other faith-based books, etc. I was at an event and when I heard the facilitator say, "we need to meet the budget," I knew that I was in trouble. Because people are going to eat, people are going to buy jewelry, clothing, etc., but books are the last thing on their minds. So, consider what you're offering, consider the crowd and then you shouldn't be disappointed at the results. Was I disappointed? Of course. Did I do my homework? Yes. Did I check all of the boxes? Yes. But I can't make people buy what I have to offer. I was used to the rules of not being open during service or day sessions, but you would have access for business on the event schedule. I obeyed the rules but when the access to business came, people weren't interested because their money was in the offering. So be aware of that. It is a part of doing business. You might be disappointed but don't be angry, show out at the event or cause problems among other vendors. Keep the faith, encourage yourself and keep moving. It's business. On the other hand, as a faith-based individual, I know GOD and HE WILL provide for me, my family and my business. There is a lesson in each and every experience. Trust me.

Notes

Coach/Speaker Platform Events

Faith-based and coach/speaker-built events are similar but not the same. The coach/speaker platform events are coach built. They have a committed audience, provided high-quality content, and their audience wants more. The coach has created an event, invited them and has invited you as a vendor. Never forget that the platform is built by that coach. Rule #1, you are invited to this platform and it's a privilege. I'll say it again, the audience is in the room or on the virtual Zoom call because of the coach or speaker. I say that twice so that you don't forget it. You are an added bonus to this platform. Be professional, gracious and understand where you are and the opportunity that you have been given. They don't have to let you be a vendor and normally, to be a speaker is invitation only or a "pay to play," which means the people on the platform paid a hefty price to be on that stage. There is no right or wrong, good or bad, but just the way it is. The host decides. You have to decide whether you are going to participate and follow the rules.

Be aware that most coaches pitch a new product or service at the event. That is also another norm. If you host your own events, you should pitch something, an offer, a new product, service, eBook, free download, a gift bag, a class or course at your own event. Let me give you an example.

For example, and I will use my two middle names, Coach Ann Kay has a large client/audience that follows her, she's consistent on social media, has offerings and decides to have an event. The event has speakers, vendors and there will be an offer at the end for people to work with Coach Ann Kay, buy her new book, take her next class or be in her mastermind for 3–6 months. Coach Ann Kay will speak at her conference. Other speakers will speak and are listed on the flyer along with their topic a link to their website. The speakers will be told what they can and cannot sell from the stage, at what price point or provide a link for email list building. The speaker/vendor is required to promote the event on their social media and must prove it by tagging the host or using the hashtag that is associated with the event. Know that there is someone on the team who is checking to make sure that the posting/sharing/commenting requirements have been completed. I'll talk more about promotion activities for vendors later, but know that this is becoming more and more important to participate as a vendor and especially, if you want to speak on the platform. As a host of in-person and virtual events, know that this is something that I watch carefully and consider prior to inviting people on my platform. Promoting doesn't guarantee that people will come, register or participate but I guarantee that no one will come unless they know about it. There are never any guarantees. Promotion is necessary and key to the success of any event. Make promotion a part of your routine no matter if you're in business full-time, part-time, sometime or one time.

I have participated as a vendor/exhibitor/speaker with a combination of any number of the above examples that I have given.

Gratefully, I have been participated at coach-built platform events and the coaches made and filled to capacity their offer, but people still joined my email list and purchased my products/services. It can happen.

I am always honored for my image and name to be on the flyer with the other wonderful speakers along with a social media graphic separately with my face, name and session title. It is rare for me to receive a vendor graphic so I normally create my own. Canva and I are best friends. Vendors may receive a mention as being in attendance but rarely are they showcased. If you go back through my social media posts, you will see my vendor posts, an itinerary and what my role will be at the event. I want to build good promotion habits for myself, my business and be a role model for my clients or those watching/following me. Additionally, a good business owner/coach should have the "do as I do" and not the "do as I say only" mentality and approach for their clients and business.

When organizations require that you apply to be a vendor at their events, that is what they are looking for. Did you promote, how active are you on social media and how many eyes have the potential to see and know about their event? It's important.

Non-Profit Events

I realize that most of you will skip this chapter and move on. Why? What is the point of going to events if you are NOT going to make some type of profit? I understand and agree with you and disagree all at the same time. Attending and participating any events should have a goal and one of those is to position yourself, your products and services to gain attention, introduction, knowledge and interest. I want you to win! I don't care what industry; I want you to win. I own a non-profit company but have focused on the "for" profit arena because it is profitable for me. I have been led to not overlook these events. For example, I recently was asked to set up a table with my products and services at a resource event along with mental health, recovery, homeless and substance abuse agencies. I primarily wouldn't be focusing on these events because the agency may have a budget but the general clientele may or may not have the money to pay for what I have to offer. I forgot that one of the main strategies of therapy is writing. In one of the lowest times of my life, I journaled for healing. I also forgot about the people who are employees, therapist and counselors of these agencies needing diverse materials for people of different backgrounds and language. I was about to leave money on the table but God made somebody put me on their mind. I showed up and it was wonderful. Remember attending events has multiple purposes and one of them is introduction. I attended the non-profit event primarily with the objective of "introduction." I wanted them to meet me, know what I do, know what I offer and THEN make a decision as to whether we needed to talk further. My total expectation was just to introduce myself and my products. There is something about being in the room that makes the difference. I left with multiple contacts and one agency got a grant and I am going to teach writing to a women's recover event. I was invited to another community event, in front of a new audience AND I sold product. Win, win and more wins. I am now on the list as a community partner and have been invited to more events in my city and surrounding area. I can't guarantee anything but if you don't show up and show out for your brand, you are not in the position to take it to the next level.

I have my own non-profit that is a 501(c)(3), www.bkroystonfoundation.org. People can make donations for my non-profit programming and receive a tax write off. This is a win for the donor and a win for the non-profit.

Next, you have to have a mindset for this industry and clientele. Your language has to change. Your methods will have to change. If you don't have the personality, call, character or heart to help people and only move for money, power and position for your own personal gain, don't do it and skip to the next chapter. This is not for you. Be honest. You need a service/servant heart and mentality, not to abuse or be used or taken advantage but to serve. If it doesn't work, it doesn't work. The mindset and mentality have to be correct, or it will always seem like a loss for you every single time. Me personally, I have a giver's heart and I know that I have to limit myself in the area because I will give away the world, my husband says so. BUT I have been so blessed that, within limits and boundaries, I can't see this community in need and not figure out a way to help. That's just me personally. If this is you and you have a heart for this audience/clientele and service, check out the following tips.

Here are some tips for a non-profit event:
1. Have a giveaway.
2. Have your promotional materials, business cards, post cards, QR code ready to go.
3. Have a clear message — Who are you? What do you do? What are you offering?
4. Keep your mind open to the possibilities and think outside of the box and the norm.
5. Follow-up is so key to the success of your participation in the event and the success that can occur even after the event is over that I have a specific section coming up about follow-up. But if there is an opportunity for you to follow up with someone you met at an event, do it as quickly as possible. Some people use 24 hours as a rule but make sure that it is within the first week after the event that you follow-

up. If it takes you a little longer starting out, make sure that it is within 30 days after the event is over. No matter if it is an email, text or phone call. Follow up and contact the new connection, potential collaboration or new customer. We'll talk about more later as to what that follow-up process or procedure should look like.

Notes

Virtual Events

Virtual events are not new and were prevalent even prior to COVID season in 2020. The preferred events, for me, have always been in-person. Most of us kept our businesses alive and moving during the pandemic with virtual events.

Questions to consider are very similar to in-person events. Who is hosting the event? What type of event is it? What day of the week, time of the day and season will the virtual event be held? What will be allowed to promote or sell or even talk about during the event? How much does it cost for participation? "Pay to play" can apply to virtual events. Even though there isn't aren't the in-person logistics, there could be a cost to participate on the host's platform. That's what "pay to play" actually means. You have to pay to be on that platform. Get used to it. The more people and access, the higher the cost can be.

What you have to offer at the event will depend on the rules and regulations of the virtual event. For example, some events only allow you to offer email list building or a free giveaway during their event. High ticket items, workshops, courses, masterminds, etc., may not be able to be pitched. Know the rules and abide by them.

Secondly, make sure that you ask how your name can be displayed in the Zoom, StreamYard or other social media platform software. If they don't care, I use my bio link site which gives people access to all of my contact information, social media handles, websites and online stores, i.e., www.juliaakroyston.com. Shameless plug. I do it often. My name is listed and the website leads to a multitude of websites and giveaways.

Next, be in a well-lit quiet space, dress nicely and have a good sound quality microphone. Smile even if the host hasn't called on you yet. Nod your head when the other speaker is talking, especially if you all are on camera. Your facial expressions matter!

Next, have cheat sheets, paper or other notes to make sure that you don't forget something. For example, your website, social media handles or elevator pitch. Remember it's virtual, no one can see what you have in your hands. Make the most of it. In the post COVID space, be sure to determine, ask or adjust your camera so that only what you want to be seen, can be seen.

Always have a sample of your product near you. If it's a t-shirt, make-up, body butters, book or other merchandise, show it. Remember live streams are normally saved the social media platform. If it's being streamed to multiple platforms, that's even better and the videos stay up even longer. Maximize the exposure.

Respond to any questions or comments directed at you during the live stream or pre-recorded interview. Then go back through the comments and respond to any comments or questions that were missed. See if you can assist with an answer or an offer.

Getting your message in front of any new audience is so critical, important and rare for new business owners. I don't want you to miss out on any opportunity.

Notes

How Much Does It Cost?

> **Sponsor/Vendor Request Form**
>
> We are thrilled you are interested in participating as a sponsor or vendor for our upcoming conference on May 10th-12th.
>
> Exhibition Hall Vendor Includes:
>
> - 10x10 booth space in exhibit hall (pipe & drape included)
>
> - Exhibit table (includes (1) 8-ft. table, (1) table cloth & (2) chairs)
>
> -2 General Admission Registrations
>
> - 2 Days of Vendor Space
>
> **$1500**
>
> We have so many amazing things planned and are happy to include you in the mix.
>
> Please complete this survey which will help us craft the best opportunity for you and your business.

Now most of you probably feel like this chapter should have been right after the chapter "The Event." I get it and you are probably right, but I needed to get some other things explained before I started talking about cost. Why? Some vending fees are worth the cost. If you save and budget for it, you can participate at some point in your business.

Some events are worth the investment. You have to determine if it is worth it for you and your business. At the beginning of the chapter, I have an image of the sponsor/vendor request form for an event. You can tell what the event is for and who the sponsor/host/promoter is on purpose. Let's evaluate it to see if it is something that we should consider participating in or not. Now, remember my earlier advice on thorough research, homework, asking other people who have participated in the event.

Most people would stop and ignore the request form at the $1500. Let's take a look. First, the event is three days, but you only have the space for two days. Now we have split the cost of the space alone, no travel, hotel or food at $750 for each day. The admission fee was $250 per person. So, the two days that we are vending is equal to the $500 for two people to participate in the conference. Therefore, the two admission tickets are a great idea but you would need two people to accompany you and attend the conference to get the full benefit from those tickets. I have multiple clients under my companies so we can split the cost that way but some events don't allow you to share space with products that don't match or multiple companies under one event name. Ask first.

Let's go back to the first number of $750 per day, which is what you need to sell to cover the cost of the vending space only. If you have a product that costs $10, you would need to sell 75 of them to make the $750 per day. If the product costs $50, you would only need to sell 15 of them to get your $750 per day. If you have an upcoming course for $500, you would need to sell two or if you sell three, that would cover all of the vending space fee.

Now, I know that you are saying, "I don't have a product that will sell enough to participate in this event." You are right, and I didn't participate in these types of events when I first started. It wasn't just because my business didn't have the money for the cost of the vending fee, but I didn't have the products, services, systems or infrastructure in place to participate in this type of event.

That's the reason I say that it is not only the vending fee that you have to look at but also how much does it cost you to prepare for this level of event. The website is ready? Do you have enough promotional materials, inventory and not to mention, the travel expenses and the follow up systems? "How much does it cost?" is not only the money but cost of doing business.

I suggest that you build UP to this type of event.

How many vendors are they expecting at this event? That is a HUGE question to ask. You need to know how many vendors you are competing with. Does the audience spend money at this event and is it truly your product's target audience? There are so many questions to ask so that it is worth it for you and your business.

Where is the event? Will it cost you $1000 to travel, stay in a hotel and eat while at the event? That is on top of the $1500 for just the booth alone.

How many people are they expecting so how much inventory should you bring? If you need to purchase 100 products at a cost of $5 each, that's already $500 more dollars to add to your budget just for this event alone. Now, if you are like me and travel a lot, participate in local events too, that might not be a big expense. But if you rarely go to back-to-back events, that inventory could be sitting in your closet, garage or storage for a minute and not sell until you decide to participate in your next event. Something to think about.

I confess that I spent $2400+ for an event once. Remember I said, "once." I saved, prepared and worked to get the vending fee. My husband wasn't happy, but I wanted to get in front of this audience. It was an international event but it was held in my city, Louisville, Kentucky.

I was a speaker on a panel and had a special, advertised "meet the author/publisher event." I could get to the venue in 15 minutes. I didn't have a hotel stay. I ate out of my refrigerator, spent a little during the day for lunch. I had to pay for parking downtown. Altogether besides the vendor fee, I probably spent $50 in parking and $50 for food. It was a week-long event. The problem is I knew that I could NOT sell on the floor, but I didn't realize how little budgets that librarians had and in spite of my follow-up, I've only been contacted by one librarian from that event. Very disappointing but the fee was written off of my taxes and I learned an expensive but valuable lesson at that event. Clearly, one and done.

Because of the products and services that I offer, the sweet spot for the cost to participate at events for me, is the $250–$300 price point, in my regional area and within one to three hours from home.

We all prefer and love events with no vendor/exhibitor fee but today it is very rare. Over the years, I have noticed that events with no vending/exhibitor fee, there may not be much attendance. If the event is free to participate, then if you only sell one thing, it is a win. For me, I take into account all of the costs for being at the event. The inventory cost, the gas to get there and my time away from something else to participate. Time is money.

If you don't sell something, come away with SOMETHING! Make a new connection, obtain some information or learning something new to use in the future. Count up the cost!

Event Rules and Regulations

Now we have talked about reading the prospectus and understanding the basics of the event, but you also have to know the specific rules of the event. The rules are things that will be or will NOT be tolerated at the event. Certain signage, loud music, setting up late, taking down early, blocking other people's tables or booths, inappropriate behavior of any kind, inappropriate products with images that are not suitable for family audiences, stealing or sabotaging other people's business, are not allowed. Now these rules are very common, and some are punishable by the law, removal from the event and even banishment from participating ever again. But there are other rules that are unique to the event. For example, having a carpet on the floor is not something that I've seen very often but it was a part of one show rule. I had to supply my own carpet for the space or pay more than $200 to rent a carpet to be within show guidelines and rules. No carpet then no set-up at the event. Another event, I was required to have a "black" table cover. The table decorations for the table were of my choosing, but the cover had to be ***black***. There are some rules that the event hosts may state but don't enforce so be ready for that too.

As a business owner, representative of my brand, and knowing that trouble travels like wild fire on social media, I follow the rules. Bad news travels fast. Don't ruin your reputation by not following the rules, being rude to or disrespecting other people's businesses. Don't do it. It matters. Opportunities can come your way because of relationships and how you treat other people. Opportunities may also come because people watch how you react and handle yourself in certain situations that may not even involve them. Follow the rules. It matters.

Communication

Communication is very important no matter the price point for the event. Prior to the payment being made, there usually is a lot of communication seeking vendors and exhibitors to help pay for the event and hopefully, help promote the event as well. Often after payment is made, there is a quick thank you email and nothing until one to two weeks prior to the event. There may be some hosts who respond to emails with questions, but the responses can be slow.

The grade for the communication from the event host or organizer, for me, is primarily given after the event is over. Don't get me wrong and, as a disclaimer, they can't tell you everything that will happen at an event. It's impossible, but the BIG, critical and crucial things that make for a successful event should be communicated. There are things that experienced hosts forget. When the question is asked, then there is another email or updated communication sent out. Now in the hosts' defense, as the vendor/exhibitor, you need to check your email often and your spam folder just in case. I confess that I have asked a question and found the answer in my email spam or junk folder. It happens, I'm human and admit the mistake. If you only check email once or twice a week, step up your game closer to the time of an upcoming event. That email could give you some valuable information or save you some money or give you greater exposure at the event, you never know. By the way, you should be aware of all of the communication outlets. If they have a private Facebook page for the event, join it. There are times that there are multiple Facebook pages for the event, specific groups and specific attendee pages as well. Don't miss out on any of the opportunities.

Next, if there is a due date for a specific response, DO IT early and don't wait until the last minute. Why? Because some opportunities are based on a "first come, first served" basis and when the space is full, it's full!

Finally, remember that communication should be two-way and work both ways. There are times that I respond to the email, "thank you." I want the host or coordinator to know that I received the information, understand and appreciate them. I have had hosts or coordinators who know me personally and ask my opinion on changes that they need to make with the event or the venue or clearly circumstances beyond their control. Why — because I respond! I am experienced and did I mention that I support, promote and paid the fee on time? That too. Now I am far from perfect but remember my friends tease me and call me the "queen of events" so I must be doing something right. Let's go!

Notes

Event Promotion

Now, this is an area that I want you to pay serious attention to. As an event host, promoter and participant, this is a topic that I strongly push for my clients and myself. I also get very irritated when I hear other vendors complain about the lack of attendance, participation, traffic and sales. My question is always, "Did you promote the event? Did you share the flyers on your social media and email list platforms? How much did you promote that you were going to be at the event?"

Yes, it is the responsibility of the host of the event to promote the event. Depending on how successful the event has been in the past, there will be attendees to the event. If it is an outside event, we may can count on passing by traffic but there are never any guarantees of traffic or sales. Promotion has to occur on both parties of the event, the promoter and the vendor. There are no options. I'm sorry, but you must promote. Share a graphic, do a video, go LIVE prior to the event and go LIVE at the event. Share pictures while at the event and later memories from the event on social media.

We mentioned earlier about approval for participation in some events based on not only your product, service, display of your set-up, but also your social media following and promotion. Remember there are some companies that check your social media before they hire you at their company. There are some companies that won't work with you, buy from you or sell to you until they have checked your social media. Promotion is not an option. Promotion is a very important key to the success of the event. If you are a vendor and didn't promote the event, no one comes or buys what you have to offer, that's not just the promoter's fault but also partly your fault. Events should be considered a partnership and you should bring what you have to the event. If you promoted and it still wasn't a very successful event, that's for a later chapter. Some questions to ask yourself are: should you have been attending this event? Was this your target audience? Did you promote and how often? This chapter is to let you know that you MUST promote just as hard as if you were hosting it yourself. It's not an option. I guess I'll move on.

What does event promotion look like?

I have attended for the past 10 years an outside festival called the Gaslight Festival. Thousands of people come each year from around the city and the surrounding areas for this outside fall festival. There are arts, crafts, custom artwork, non-profits, politicians come through who are running for office, kids' area, food, fun, the businesses along the layout are open and spotlighting their products and services, well attended and very secure. The police and sheriff's departments both work together and are very present to ensure the safety and security of this family event. There is a website, links to register electronically, and a full packet with the map and other information along with the festival layout. The booths are pre-assigned, with free parking for vendors; there are plenty of volunteers to help each vendor set up and break down. It is very organized and well run. I didn't know how important this event was until I went to another event and realized how spoiled I was at Gaslight.

There is always local promotion, television promotion, each vendor is given promotional flyers, etc. If the weather is good or bad, people come out, attend and support.

The flyers of where the booth is and the people who will be participating at my booth.

See below:

Here is the flyer for the live stream event prior to the event below.

Here is my monthly flyer of where my husband and I will be travelling to.

As you can see, the Gaslight Festival is on the list.

Meet Brian and Julia

Gaslight Festival, Jeffersontown, KY
September 13 - 15

Life Spring Health Event, Clarksville, IN
September 21

Annual Harvest Bazaar - Louisville, KY
September 28th

Writing Workshop - Louisville, KY
Gye Namye Bookstore - October 5

MANC Raleigh Conference Raleigh, NC
October 11-12

I also put the flyers on my Facebook header, which I also use as a billboard of my upcoming events or new releases or other announcements.

See an examples below:

I also go live every Sunday morning at 9:30 from my Facebook @juliaaroyston and YouTube Channel @bkroystonpublishing to empower and inspire people but also give my weekly and monthly announcements of where I will be in the upcoming week.

Finally, I also send these announcements, advertisements, flyers and updates to my email list. I don't just tell you to do it, I have receipts of doing it myself for my business, products, services and upcoming events. I promote the event far in advance. Sometimes people are there because they saw the event flyer or other promotion on my social media pages.

To stay connected with me, visit www.connectwithroyston.com. Let's go!

How long should you promote?

I'm glad you asked, as soon as the event is finalized, you have registered and paid the vendor fee, you should begin promoting. "Save the Date," "I'll be here," "Join me here" or "I'm here" announcements coming all along the event promotion journey.

JOIN US - LET'S GO!

MARCH ON!

There will be times that I create my own vendor flyer based on the host's flyer. This was an attendee flyer, but I changed it to be a vendor flyer. I know that they didn't care because it promoted the event highly.

Or this one

I realize that some of you may be thinking, "Julia, that is too much." But when you attend an event and you realize that you have promoted via all of the avenues, outlets and platforms that you have access to, it is a very comforting feeling. Even if the event doesn't turn out or render the results like I want, I am still at peace that I did all that I could do to help push, promote and publicize the event to success. There are no guarantees, but I guarantee you that the event and your outcomes will be better if you promote.

If you need promotion help, let's have a conversation at www.talkwithroyston.com. Let's go and PROMOTE!

The Offer

I look at each event as a part of my introduction, sales, email list building and promotional journey. Each event has potential, to lead to a customer or client. That's why I go to the event: it is one of my goals. Each event that I attend plays a part of building my business, exposing people to me, my products and services. So, the first thing I do is go back to the event prospectus, flyer or other advertisement and go through the steps that I have outlined in this book. First, who is the host, what is the event, when, where and the season of the event and who have they targeted to be at the event. That's always first.

Next, I check my inventory of books, upcoming events, workshops and classes that I have scheduled and figure out what all I have to offer.

The first thing that people see when they're at my table or at an event is my books. Next, they meet me and find out who I am. Next, they determine whether they want to buy the book and stay in connection with me even after the event is over.

Since they are at the table, I let them know that I coach, teach, speak and a full-service publisher. I can help them write their own books and can speak to a group to help them write, publish or promote their books. Remember we are talking about the offer in this chapter. The offer is everything that you have going on in addition to what is on your table. If you don't offer classes yet, at least get their information to stay in contact for the next event or when you are offering classes, retreats or attending other events in the area. Getting people's information to stay in touch kept my business alive during the pandemic and beyond.

Stop right here, think and write below what you have to offer:

_____
_____
_____
_____
_____
_____
_____
_____
_____
_____
_____
_____
_____
_____
_____
_____
_____
_____

Here is my list:

Books to purchase

Books to giveaway

Books online to sell in bulk

Contact information to host Book Fairs

Music CDs

T-shirts

Writing or Business Coaching Services

Publishing Services

Technology and Promotional Services

Upcoming Events that I am attending or hosting

Networking opportunities for my For Profit and Non-Profit Business

I will have all of my promotional materials to stay connected with me and/or purchase my books.

Take the time to really think about what you will offer on your table or booth before the next event. Don't forget to remember the organizations for which you volunteer your time, church events, etc. You may not get in front of this particular audience again so take advantage of the opportunity. With the review of everything that you do, participate in and provide though your business, you could discover that you have more to offer than you know.

Notes

The Giveaway

Giveaways are designed to attract people to your table/booth. I don't do a giveaway each and every time, but if it is an audience that I really want to do business with and it is my first time there, I will offer a giveaway. It may be product, technology or a gift card.

You may want to consider having a giveaway that goes along with the theme of the event, the likes and/or needs of the audience or some other creative giveaway that is attractive and desirable. In the past, when I had only a few of my product to sell, I would have candy, mints or other sweets to give a way. I don't have much room on my table for candy but if there will be little children at an event, candy always works.

There are some events that require a giveaway and that is fine because you know that at least one person has your product in their hand.

In addition to the contact information that you receive on your own, there are other event hosts that give you the list of attendees. I love to attend these events but the price point is higher because you are in essence paying for the list of attendees. Watch out for scam artists who say that they are selling you a list of attendees but I only get the list from the actual host of the event and not a third party; it is usually a scam. You'll have a list of names, but they may not even have attended the event or be your target audience or even interested in what you have to offer. It makes a difference. If people don't buy from you, that's fine but, at least, you want to stay connected and know about what you have to offer and be a part of the target audience that you want to reach in the future.

The Vendor/Exhibitor Team

Let me be totally transparent for a moment. I realize that this is a business book, and I am about my business, but I have God in my business. I have trust issues and control issues. That's me, my truth and I own it. Only God is omnipresent and everywhere at the same time so I can't do it all. As my business friends told me repeatedly, "Julia, you can't grow or scale alone. You must have a team."

My feelings were hurt, I gave them a sad look on my face and let out a huge sigh but admitted that they were right. In my mind I said, "But I've built this brand with God, myself and family. My family loves and supports me greatly, but they have other projects, agendas and lives to tend to and can't be with me and my business all of the time. Lord, send me a team. Even if it is temporary, Lord send me people that I can trust and work with." He did just that. Now, I understand that as much as I love and trust them, there are times when they have other plans, emergencies, families, illnesses and previous obligations to attend. I get that but I wouldn't trade my team for anything. What does it take to have a great vendor/exhibitor team?

Teachable

Yes, this is first. If you know everything and I can't tell, teach or train you about my products, services, brand or procedures, then I don't need you. I know that is harsh but true. There are some events that I only get one shot to make a connection, network or make a sale. Event fees are too expensive so I can't mess up that one shot with people that won't listen. I may struggle and be exhausted, but it might be best that I attend by myself along with my husband. I know I am supposed to be scaling, but if you're on my team, you represent me and my brand when I'm not around. I will text or call to check in and know that other people will snitch. It could be another vendor or customer but they tell. I will know how the event went even if I'm not there. The customers will tell me, email me, text me or inbox me on social media. I will find out. Fortunately, I only hear great things.

The Goal and Objective

I have a friend who often reminds me when people try to get me off course, "We write, publish and sell books over here." I laugh and get right back on course.

When you're multi-gifted, people try to drag you back to where you were and want to see you only in a previous place, position or capacity. They loved the old you and want you to remain right there. I have sung since I was eight years old and will sing, if called upon and released by God. If you've known me more than 25 years, you met me as a singer, songwriter, recording artist and only had written one to three books. The gifted are normally on the move, using, developing, blessing others and being blessed by their gift. It's not a bad thing, it's just how people perceive you, love you and don't want you to move out of that space. Let that bless you.

Train everyone on your team what the goals and objectives are for the business. When the team starts to remind you of the goals and objectives then you know you've got a great team. When they can tell you what your mission, vision and objectives are back to you, take care of that team.

A Positive Personality

People are easily attracted to people with a great personality. When we are at an event that's the type of people that I need with me; those that attract. There are those who are at events and they consider the event a failure because they didn't sell much product. As one who observes people and has had experience at events, sometimes the real problem is the products but the withdrawn and unattractive personality of the person at the table or booth. It has nothing to do with the outward appearance or looks but it has everything to do with what is going on inside of them. We've established that looking down at a cell phone is a "no no," but another one for me is not smiling or not standing up when the potential customer comes to the table. Another problem I have, is not asking questions, giving compliments or inquiring to the needs, wants and desires of the potential customer. Some people you can tell need space and just want to browse. Jumping right into conversation or asking questions or showing someone a specific product should be done slowly and carefully. Over time, I can get a feel for how to approach people and how to engage. Now sometimes I'm wrong, off target or miss it but I let the customer guide me. Some people walk up and start specifically going to a specific product and I usually always speak and say hello. I notice the person for a second and then add, "If you have questions, let me know or if you need help, let me know." Keep smiling, keep observing and keep engaging, if necessary, the whole time. Keep your eye on them, observe their movement and be ready with any questions, especially, "How much is this?" There will be people who buy immediately after you tell them the price. Others will walk away. No matter how people walk by and buy nothing, be consistent and then watch someone buy what you have to offer. Some people look at every booth, count their money and if they walked away, may come back and buy on their way. Keep smiling. Keep speaking. Keep paying attention and be ready.

Professionalism and Character

Character in my definition is striving to do the right thing when no one is listening or looking at the person. You may make an honest mistake but even if a mistake is made, you own it, we correct and do better next time. With character, we can trust. Can I trust you with my products and sales? If I am away from the table or booth in the bathroom, can I trust you to collect the money AND get it to me? Can I trust you speaking with a potential customer and making an impact, not necessarily a sale? Get this in your mind. Being personable and looking professionalism is wonderful but without character, I can't trust you and you can't be on the team.

On the other hand, check your character as the business owner, leader and CEO of your operation or business. Can the team trust you? Can the team depend on you? Will you treat them well, fairly and with respect without being demeaning, talking to them harshly and making them feel unappreciated? It works both ways. I own Book Business Boss Consulting and want everyone to show up as a "boss" in their business, but that doesn't mean that you treat people any kind of way. Whether a customer or team member — it does matter how they are being treated. Handle your business but be sure and take special care of your people who are working with you to help you be the boss of your business and life.

Knowledge of the Products and Services

Be sure to give your team ample opportunity to learn about your products and services. The team needs to know the ingredients, backstory, benefits and price of the products at any event.

At large events, there are multiple people asking at the same time about the products and services that you have on the table or in the booth. If someone is on your team, they should be as informed as possible. Now there may arise questions that need to be deferred to you but overall, everyone should know about the core products, services and their prices. You may offer a test, quiz or review of the products prior to going to a live event. Don't be in such a hurry to have help and not prepare the help or assistants for success on both sides, you and the customer.

Work Ethic

Now this is the second, I don't need you. If I have to beg you to work and pay you too, I don't need you. Some people working with me have a work ethic that matches mine, which is a lot.

Event Checklist

By now, you realize that I am an author, publisher, consultant, etc., and my product is books. My ultimate goal is for you to use the advice in this book for any industry area, no matter what you sell.

The event checklist in this section will need to be tweaked based on what your business, brand, products and services. There are events that I need more of one product over another product, an extra table, an extra portable battery charger for my phone and more pens, bags, etc. I've learned to take more than I need of everything that will fit in the car or truck. I've also learned from my experience and my clients, who remind me of things and questions that I need to ask at an event. I love getting to know new people and I need to be as prepared for the connection, the sale and the follow-up.

After my research, I can go in assuming the set-up but over time, I realize that I have to be prepared for the unexpected.

I can't tell you every, single thing that you are going to need for your business, products or services but I suggestion that you review my list, see what works for you and then make a list of your own. Start with the basics and your budget and then as you sell, make additions to what you need for a successful event.

Turn the page, let's go!

Attitude

Now I know that you thought the first thing was going to be inventory but whether I am going to an event across the street, across town or the country, I check my attitude. I want to be positive. I need to get enough rest. Go to bed early. Eat a good balanced diet. You've got to take care of your body so that you can present yourself, products and services in the best light. Remember to smile. Be talkative. Engage with as many people as possible who come near you, your table or booth. It is important. Find something that you can compliment someone on and make eye contact. You may be hoarse at the end of the day, but it will be worth it. If you are attending a multi-day event, when I'm back at the hotel, I seek to rest my voice so I can talk to more people the next day. It keeps my attitude in check and keeps me with a positive outlook no matter the outcome.

Position

No matter your booth selection, table position or access to the entrance of the event, position yourself from behind the table to gain greater access to the customer. If you are in a very tight space and can't stand in front of your table or booth, always stand up and give your undivided attention to the potential customer.

People enjoy and appreciate the attention. If your head is down in your phone, they will walk on by you. Oops, you missed a sale. If you are at an event with 50–100 or more vendors, the competition is stiff and you've got to bring your "A" game to the event. Don't sleep on any customer because oops, you may miss another sale. Bathroom breaks are essential but that's the reason you have an assistant or a team member so that money is not left on the table and you miss a potential sale. "Money left on the table" is a phrase in business that means that the product is left on the table, or your offer was not sold. No money exchanged hands, and the product or offer was left on the table and not money in your pocket.

Customer Service

There will be times that someone will contact you during and even after the event is over. Respond. I've had people go to back to their hotel room, go through their bags, the vendor list in the program book or business cards and start reaching out to the people they met that same day. I reap respond.

When I make a sale and hand the customer the bag, I remind them that my contact information is inside the bag and that they can reach out to me after the event if there is a question, problem or possibly, they'll want to buy more. It has happened. I promise you and it was wonderful for my business and budget. Be sure and respond.

Customer Service Matters.

Appreciation

"Thank you," "have a great day," or "blessings to you" or "we appreciate your support," are still wonderful words that are not only polite but show appreciation to the customer and can leave a lasting impression. I guarantee that if you attend that same event another year, someone will remember you just because of your appreciation, customer service, position, access and attitude. Don't forget about these small details that can make a huge difference.

Inventory

What are you selling? No matter if you are at a large trade show or a farmer's market, have plenty of what you're selling. If you sell out, wonderful! BUT if you sell out, get in the habit of taking orders, get the money, their contact information and ship it to them later. This is especially helpful at large trade shows where people have limited space in their luggage.

Plan, plan and plan again how much inventory that you should have on hand. Know how much inventory you need to purchase. There are times that I am at an event, running low, not quite sold out but I'll place an order on the spot. Why? Because I may have events coming up and know that the audience at the future events want or need what I am selling. Be prepared and plan ahead. I realize that there are some events that come up at the last minute but strive to always have product on hand at all times. My clients know that is Rule #1.

Table Covers

I have used king size sheets, queen size sheets, tablecloths, custom cut material from the fabric store and a combination of all of the above. These days, I have covers for 6-foot and 8-foot tables. My brand colors are black, red and white but I focus on black and red. Black covers are for elegance, and it doesn't show spots. People set down food and drinks on the table and even if they have clean hands, they can cause stains that don't always come out after washing. There are some events that require black table covers so be sure and check the Vendor Requirements. If not listed as a requirement, ask.

I like utilizing the linens and the covers that the event hosts provide better because I don't have to use mine and thus avoid the wear and tear on my table covers. My next big investment is to have my brands on my table cover. In the meantime, I have table runners which I'll talk about later.

Take a look.

Example of a 10 x 10 Booth Set-Up, below:

Examples of Branded Table Covers

Table Runner

A table runner is a cover in the middle of the front of the table that works really well and can be easily cleaned. I have also used other banners, my branded t-shirts and even one of my branded backpacks for the front runner of the table, see below.

Signage

I started out with little to no signage. Over time and much savings, I was able to purchase not one but multiple banners.

Early on, I just put my picture in a picture frame as signage. It was a start and I encourage people to start where you start. Your budget has to always be considered. Don't try to keep up with other people. Do what you can do and make sure that it is neat, presentable and if the people want what you have, they will buy it. In the picture below, the lady in the blue sweater coat with her wallet in her hand ready to buy and she did.

No signage, just product

In this picture, I had little signage just product. I let my smile and greeting be the signage.

My early on —— Crossbow Banners

The banner collapsed into three pieces, and I had to roll up the banner with the information on it.

I have had signage on tripods, which I don't use much these days but definitely did early on in my career. I purchased motivational signs to add to my table especially since I didn't have many books back then to attract people to my table. When I have the time, money and energy, I do put candy on the table to attract people as well. But early on, I realized that people ate the candy and didn't buy what I had to offer.

Retractable Banners

Most of the time and not all of the time, signage is included with the booth or table fee. There are all types of signage from top signs over a skirted booth to signs placed on top of the table to just a piece of paper that identifies which company has been assigned to which booth. As for BK Royston Publishing, I come with signage of my own.

Retractable banners are extremely popular, and I have seen so many variations of what to put on the banner it is not funny. The most important thing for me is your logo, social media handles and contact information. Design is up to you. I have seen banners that spotlight certain products, services and dated material. I spotlighted those things when I first started out and that was a mistake, but I didn't know any better. I was new and still really building my brand and credibility as a business owner and publisher.

Now, the store is open! See below.

I have two retractable banners especially when I am at outside events. The Julia A. Royston banner is primarily used when I am a speaker and my own books, and the BK Royston Publishing Stores Banner covers everything else.

Table Banners

Because of all of the things that I have to travel with, there are some events that I use tabletop banners. Tabletop banners are much smaller, lighter in weight and much easier to travel with and set up. I have also seen these banners at more events which saves on time, luggage and stress on your body.

Tabletop sign of me and my information.

Tabletop sign of Terrance the Terrific and the young adult/tween section

Table Signs organize my products.

Book Fair Posters and Signage

Tabletop banner for BK Royston Foundation
www.bkroystonfoundation.org

A step and repeat banner for branding and pictures of multiple businesses.

Pens

I use a multiplicity of pens. Why? Because the ink can run out without warning. As an author, I like to sign my books and the readers love to get my signature. It's a "win win" situation. I advise you always have a Sharpie on hand in addition to multiple ink pens for taking notes, signing your products or keeping records for future communication. Do you have a pen on you? Always.

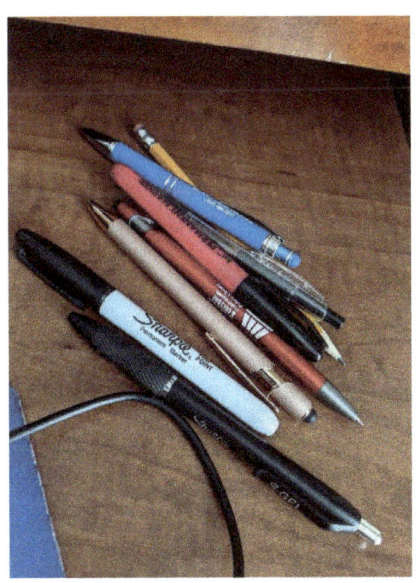

Sign-In Sheet

Even with electronic ways to sign up for my email list and for future communication, I keep a hard copy sign-in sheet. Why? Because I can make notes on the paper version. Also, when people submit their contact information, it is permission for them to be on my email list. I don't abuse this privilege with a 50-email funnel but I do communicate on a monthly basis to those who want to stay connected.

Notebooks

I am old school and want to make notes for myself about what I should remember from the event by hand. I have made some connections that weren't on my sign-in sheet. I take notes so that I can remember why I need to reach out, network or hopefully, do business together.

Change

I would say 85% of people pay with some form of electronic payment but I still carry cash with me. Why? Because there are some people who still pay in cash. When you review your inventory, you will know how much and what denominations of change to have. My products normally cost $10, $15, $20+, etc. So, I normally carry 5 and 10-dollar bills.

Depending on the city and the event, I have used all payment methods, i.e., cash, credit card, Venmo, PayPal, Zelle and Cash App. The larger the city or event, the more payment methods I use.

 I admonish you to be prepared to take more than one and up to three payment methods. Don't leave money on the table because you were unprepared. Expand your horizons and more importantly, be prepared.

Promotional Materials

I realize that digital, business cards and promotional materials are popular but not always feasible. I still come in contact with a generation that wants the card in their hand. Yes, I have the digital card and can access it on my phone but I never leave home without physical business cards, brochures, thank you cards or other promotional cards. Why? There are some people that still want the card in their hand.

Thank you cards with my contact information and ways to purchase my products have become popular and necessary as well.

Business Cards

This card is also included in my email signature just in case people don't remember me.

Display Stands

I have seen all types of ways to display products at events. I've seen small shelving, baskets, plastic bins turned upside down and covered, bowls, buckets to plates. You name it, I've seen it. It all depends on what you're selling but have a way to make it visible from afar. Suspend products up off of the table in some way so that it is attractive to people and draws them to you. There is no right or wrong way. Make sure that it is an attractive. For me, the art or picture stands have worked for my books, promotional materials, posters, etc. I have lent them out to other vendors, authors or exhibitors at events so that their products are more visible and not positioned flat on the table. Get a few or a lot but make it part of your business expense at events.

Large Stands

Small Stands

Results

The Extras

My husband is retired from a Fortune 20 company and was in their IT/Technology department for 32 years. So, cables, batteries, extension cords, power strips and an extra phone (old phones that work with just WIFI) are high on his list of extras. I helped more than one vendor with something that I had. Even extra bags, a stapler, scissors, notebook or whatever, I have shared. When I mentioned in an earlier chapter about making friends with other vendors, this helps greatly.

Sanitizer for cleaning my hands and extra cables just in case one goes bad. I promise, it has happened.

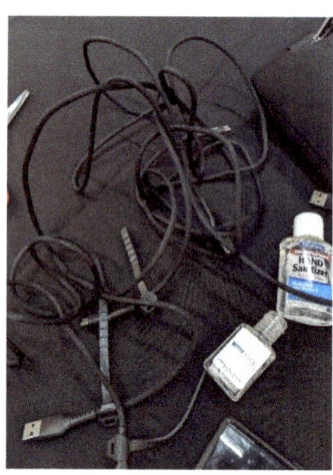

An extra battery for charging my phone when I didn't buy electricity from the event host or was not near or guaranteed to be near a plug.

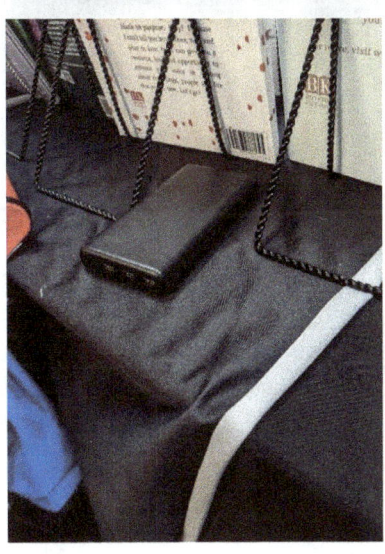

Cart

Now the cart has been a game changer, life and body saver in so many ways. I bought the first one for $200 on Amazon.com and the last one for $79 at Walmart. It doesn't matter. I now have three carts because I have so much product and accessories to carry. Large tradeshows, outside festivals or loading docks make rolling carts essential and not an option. I realize that you say, "I don't have that much to sell," but as you get older, your body is going to scream for a cart. Make that an essential business expense. Take a look.

For extra tables needed for larger trade show events.

For just everything to be carried in at one time. This is a heavy load with four containers, banner bag and my purse on top but it worked.

I carry rolling luggage, too, alongside of my carts for even more things to transport. As your business grows, you will know that I told you the truth.

Look at the picture below. To the left of the main table, it looks like we have a small table cover with a black tablecloth with a few books on top. In actuality, this is a cart with two containers on it, covered with a tablecloth to look like a table because an additional table would not fit but we had a lot of books. Credit goes to Brian Royston for this idea. Where there is a will, there is a way! As long as it is no fire hazard and the other vendors are fine around you and doesn't block anything, be creative. Let's go!

On the street, waiting for my husband to bring the card.

Notes

Travel Tips

Below are just some tips for travel. This book is much longer than I ever anticipated but felt that it is important to give you as much help as possible at events.

- Get plenty of rest.
- If possible, stay in the hotel of the event.
- If not in the event hotel, stay in a hotel that as close as possible to the event.
- Try to arrive a day early before the event if possible. If the event is later in the day, arrive early to get rest and then arrive early to the event location.
- If set-up time is from 12–5, try to arrive at 11:45 and wait so that if the booths/tables are NOT assigned, you can pick a good spot.
- Bring light snacks or a cooler if allowed, for drinks especially if the hours are more than three hours long and especially, if you are at an outside location.
- Wear comfortable shoes, clothing, etc.

- Get a cart – Walmart, Target, Online at Amazon.com
- Have a great working phone for GPS and taking electronic payment.
- MAKE FRIENDS AT THE EVENT. Yes, I am yelling and will yell it out again. BE NICE TO THE PEOPLE AROUND YOU AND MAKE FRIENDS. You just never know.
- All events do not provide free Wi-Fi. What will happen if the Wi-Fi is NOT free, and you have to accept electronic payment? Do you have a data plan to handle these transactions? This is an expense of business. Prepare for using your data just in case the Wi-Fi is NOT free. The cost of Wi-Fi can be anywhere from $10–20 per day or a few hundred dollars for some locations. Ask, evaluate and then prepare some more for the upcoming event. If your business transactions depend on Wi-Fi, prepare ahead of time.
- Smile and Have Fun.

Things Not Mentioned in the Event Application, Description or Rules and Regulations

There are additional questions that you should ask regarding things that are not listed on the inquiry form, landing page or Eventbrite information for the event. Will there be access to free or paid Wi-Fi? Are there electrical outlets nearby the vending area for access or do we have to purchase electricity. One event I attended, the electricity cost $1500. Fortunately, the booth organizers placed the electrical outlet on the edge of my booth and it was a $1500 blessing. On the layout of the vending area, how close are you to the bathrooms, food, entryways, exits, loading dock? Will there be after hours and during show security? Also, double check the exact size of the booth area. If the booth space is 10 feet by 10 feet, only bring items that will fit in a 10 foot by 10-foot space and that will not block someone else's booth on either side. With a large trade show, you may be sharing a curtain with a vendor behind you, so don't assume that you can attach displays on the curtain divider because you may not have access to it. Or even worse, it may fall down if you attach something to it. Ask first.

Unmet Expectations

I have friends that always say, "what is your goal for this event?" What is your goal for this month, quarter or year? Truthfully, I have a goal in my mind but have trouble putting it down because I don't want to be limited. On the other hand, I try to have positive and attainable goals for each event. Some events exceed my expectation and others have disappointed me greatly. I want you to understand the realities of business, the market and events. I've said it before and I'll continue to say it, it's all a risk. No matter how much planning you do, research and preparation, there may be some things that happen that the host/promoter didn't know and couldn't have planned. Emergencies and pandemics happen and we have to make adjustments. On the other hand, this is business, and we have to be prepared for what may or may not happen. My prayer is always that people sell out or recoup their investment and never have an event failure. I wouldn't wish that on my worst enemy. There are times that your expectations are not met. It's life but how do we handle it?

Let's talk about it.

No Attendees

I have been to events where there was low attendance and low sales. I have only been to one show in my life so far that no one showed up to the event. No customer came. No one. Not one. Now it is one thing to go to an event and not sell anything. I've done that and I was a participant in the event, sang, taught, etc. and still no one bought anything. That's an attendee, budget issue. They didn't have the money for what I was offering, I get it. I have been at an event and the turnout is low and/or they don't buy from you, but they bought from someone else. I get that, too.

But when you drive nine hours, spend money for two nights in a hotel, food and gas and no one shows to even see what I have to offer!? That was a first and hopefully, the only time that happens. Yes, I had participated with the host/promoter many times and he was as disappointed as I was and couldn't believe that no one showed up to his event.

What do you do when your expectations are NOT met? How do you recover for that type of loss? Well, you have to know that this is a part of doing business. I can write the loss off of my business expenses. That doesn't give me back my time and money that I invested. I can't count the loss until the end of the year but it is something rather than completely nothing. I realize that some people reading this may do your business on the side and haven't registered and incorporated your business so for you it might not be a write off but a loss. You hope that the next event will a HUGE win and will make up for that loss, but you have to acknowledge the loss as it stands. It happened. You took a risk, and it didn't turn out as you expected. Clearly, unmet expectations. But what do you do?

First, I turned it into a photoshoot and video opportunity. I am a librarian by training and nature, and this is a historical moment that I want to forget but won't ever forget and/or want to repeat. Do not take a picture of the lack of a crowd or talk about how many products were sold but spotlight on the products themselves. Take a picture of your table set-up. Take a picture of all of the other vendors and their table set-ups. Go live and talk about the products that you have to offer and drive them to your online store and/or website. Promote the people at the event while you're still there rather the event.

Next, go to every vendor table and get their cards, ask them about their products, services and what they have displayed. This gives you information about others, ideas for display at your next event, keeps them in practice of their elevator pitch and explanation of their products and services as well as an opportunity to network.

Next, at the event that no one showed, I started interviewing vendors at the event for my show and podcast. We had time, it was an opportunity, and I had the technology. The event was cut short so the business cards and promotional materials I collected were used to contact them later for interviews.

No Inventory

Now, I have had clients who ordered their products too close to the show and the inventory didn't arrive in time. I hate that because people are normally impulse buyers and normally don't buy online after the show so having product on hand is key. If the inventory doesn't show, you use it as an email list building event. Even if I ship product to an event, I always throw at least 6 books in the bag if I am travelling. Another rule of thumb is if you are getting low on product, under 10, order then and don't wait until you are totally out of product. I am reviewing my inventory and ordering while I am still at the previous event.

Display whatever sample or picture of your product that you have and talk, talk and talk some more. Take orders and pitch, pitch and pitch some more about your product, its benefits and how it can help your potential client. Get their information and then pitch to them online.

Have people open up their social media on their phone and follow you and learn more about your products and services.

Conduct a giveaway. Gift cards are everywhere. Have a sign-up sheet, raffle or another way to collect the information, pick a person and give it away. You have the contact information so you can sell to them again in the future.

Terrible Placement on the Floor

I have rarely been to an event where there wasn't foot traffic to where I was set up. But if I am too far away from traffic, I will ask if there is another space that I can move to especially if a vendor/exhibitor doesn't show up. It's rare but it has happened and I was able to move to a better spot. Now, this will NOT be the case if you were able to select your spot ahead of time. If it does happen, raise an issue and prove your point with the email confirmation of your booth or table placement.

Once it looked like I was far away from the action, but at that event, I was actually at the front door and entrance to the majority of the sessions and people couldn't miss me.

At a major street festival, I was moved and placed at the other end of the street. I was

NOT happy until I realized that there were more people and my target audience at the new spot than I had ever gotten access to all along. I was actually in the WRONG spot for multiple years. GOD and somebody on the team were looking out for me. I am eternally thankful. I put on the survey information at the end of the event, please keep me in the same end of the street, thank you.

Without getting in front of anyone else's booth and staying in your own space, get from behind the table and speak to the people walking by.

Even if they are in a hurry and have to get someone, invite them to come back and see you. Hand them a flyer or a business card on their way.

There is opportunity to meet people in the bathroom, at the water dispenser, at the restaurant or the continental breakfast line. Ladies, this is for you. Where there is a will, there is a way. Find a way. Bring people to your table or booth and then talk, talk and talk some more.

Finally, take time to reflect on everything that did happen. Determine if something could have been done that didn't happen that could have changed the event and made it more successful.

Most people blame the host/promoter and make it their fault and should have done this or that. The leader is always the first person that people are going to blame. On a side note, if you plan to host events, be prepared for this even if the event is a HUGE success and people were there in the hundreds. There will ALWAYS be somebody who thought it should have been "this or that" and they could have done it better. Let us know after you host your first event how it works out for you.

There also could have been some other factors that weren't taken into account the six months to a year the event was being planned. Did the city sponsor a new event that took some of the attendees away from your event? Was it the weather? Was it traffic, construction, roadblock or accident? Did the economy crash? Did the stock market do something? Was there another natural disaster that altered the event? Ask people who had events planned and paid for what happened during the pandemic. Most of those hosts didn't get refunds and if they did, it wasn't for the full amount.

I paid to attend an event in March of 2020. It didn't happen, I requested a refund and the host refused to give a refund because they didn't get a refund. Think first, evaluate first, reflect first before you criticize. Every successful business owner has at least 10 stories of an event, product, project, contract or client that didn't go right or well. It is a part of doing business. I guarantee you that you will learn more from failures and lessons than you ever will by success. Success spoils you. Failure teaches you.

Media Attention

I don't know what it is about me, my products or my set-up, but I have been interviewed on the spot for television, newspapers and other digital outlets on several occasions. It doesn't happen at every event, and I never know in advance, but I strive to be prepared. My husband and I, as well as my team, normally wear matching brand shirts. This draws attention to us as well as the number of products in the booth. Looking at the display, it is impressive and at times, overwhelming.

If members of the media approach me, I always say "yes" and get their card or information to follow-up and say thank you. Even if it airs outside of my viewing area and I have to check out the website to see it, I say thank you. The same applies to media attention just like virtual events, be prepared. Be ready to talk about your products or services within 30 seconds or less. Answer the questions that they ask and be prepared to give the link to your website, online store or social media.

Just like for virtual events, smile, be pleasant and speak up. Don't shy away from the microphone. This maybe local, regional or national media attention. It's your time to shine. It's your opportunity, don't miss it. Be ready so that you don't have to get ready. Point to your products. Know the link of your services and enjoy the moment. You worked for it, now bask in it!

Finally, follow-up with the media outlet or personality. Share the video or broadcast on your social media. Thank the interviewer. Thank the promoter/host for the opportunity. Check and respond to any comments.

The Follow-Up

If you are really serious about your business, follow up. You've got to take the time, make the time, schedule the time to follow up with whom you met at the event. I emphasis the follow-up even more if it is your first time at an event. Why because first impressions are lasting impressions and you never know what can happen and who the person that you are communicating with is connected to. This might be a test, a divine appointment, a divine connection or an angel, I don't know but you have to follow up. It is a part of the basic business function. I don't care how much money you make ordinarily or didn't make at the event, follow up.

It is often said that the high end, expensive brands, do not advertise. They are advertising in some way even if it is phone, email or snail mailings, etc. They are reaching out to let people know about the latest product that they have to offer. Now, it may be an exclusive list but there is someone, somewhere reaching out to the rich and famous. Don't be fooled by that. So, you may not have a multi-million-dollar brand but if you are offering anything, from food to jewelry, follow up.

My follow-up starts with a public thank you via social media. It can be private via an email, phone call, inbox, etc. but I follow up.

See below some samples of the follow-up emails and posts that I have sent out over the years. Let's go!

Social Media Thank You

Thank You Post

The Event Host/Promoter — Survey

Survey.

If the event host sends out a survey, complete the survey. I normally want to tell the host how the event went even if I have been attending for many years. I want them to know what worked and be very gracious about what didn't work.

Attendees who stopped by your booth

Email Subject: It was a pleasure meeting you at Magnolia Mall in Florence, SC

As per our conversation, I would love to interview you for my Message Motivator Podcast. Please schedule a time that is convenient at www.talkwithroyston.com. Thank you again.

It was a pleasure meeting you in the Magnolia Mall in Florence, SC. As per our conversation, visit www.juliaroystonstore.com to purchase Xavier which is Book #3 of the Men of Roberts Junction as well as any books in the Women of the Fellowship Series or any other books that I have written. If you have any questions, don't hesitate to reply to this email. Blessings. Peace. Safety.

It was a pleasure meeting you in the Magnolia Mall in Florence, SC. As per our conversation, you have an interest in writing and I have a 3-hour writer's workshop on Saturday, November 13 at 11:00 a.m. to 2:00 p.m. EST. Register for $21 at www.bkroystonpublishing.com/classes. If you have any questions or need additional information, don't hesitate to reply to this email. Blessings. Peace. Safety. Thank you!

It is always a pleasure meeting new people at huge conferences. I know that we talked about a lot of things but the best way for me to serve you is to have a conversation. To schedule a conversation, visit www.talkwithroyston.com. If you see a time that works, don't hesitate to reply to this email address and let's schedule something that works in the evening around your schedule. I look forward to speaking with you soon. I am a retired educator, but I haven't forgotten about the rigors of the educational industry. I trust that you had a great Thanksgiving holiday and hold on, the December holidays and breaks are just around the corner.

See the picture attached to remember me. Let's go!

It was a pleasure meeting at KIPP School. I trust that you are well. Let's have a conversation. Schedule a time that works at www.talkwithroyston.com. Blessings. Peace. Safety.

I am Julia Royston owner of BK Royston Publishing. I would love information regarding being a vendor for your school district. The online children's bookstore is www.roystonchildrenbookstore.com and I am a registered business for the state of Indiana. If we could schedule a conversation, visit www.talkwithroyston.com or simply reply to this email. I look forward to hearing from you soon.

It was a pleasure meeting you at Day 4 of the 2022 COGIC Women's Convention in Orlando, FL. As per our conversation, you are either interested in writing, at the beginning stages of writing and need more guidance or completed a manuscript and need next steps. I am happy to help.

Other Vendors/Exhibitors

In my travels, it is always a pleasure meeting so many incredible business owners. I am unable to purchase everyone's product or sign up for their services, but I offer my platforms, "Live Your Best Life" on www.envision-radio.com or the "Book Business Bosses Podcast" at www.bookbusinessbosspodcast.com to business owners I meet.

I would love to interview you and spotlight your business on my show. If interested, email me your picture and bio and then schedule a time at www.juliaroystoninterview.com.

Don't Eat Up Your Seed

I am not a farmer. I was bit raised on a farm. I do know the law of seed, sowing and then harvest. It is a law. You can't reap a harvest without sowing something into the ground. You can't have inventory or the vending fee if you have nothing left over or you spend every dime that you made after the event.

This is a difficult discussion, something people don't want to talk about but one that is really important for the success of your business. You must financially reconcile each event. What did you spend to get there? What did you spend on inventory or product to take with you? Did you drive the product or ship the product to the venue? What was the vending fee? What was the cost of parking at the event? What was the cost of food while you were at the event? What else did you spend while you were at the venue, city or state?

Let's look at the numbers:

Vending Fee plus Parking: $320

Travel to the 2-day event, hotel, gas, etc.

$125 per night hotel with tax: $300

Gas to travel there and back: $100

Food while in the city for 3 days including at the venue: $200

Inventory cost: $500

Total: $1420

Amount of Product Sold: $1000

Loss on the event: $420

Now if you had inventory already in stock and didn't have to buy additional inventory, I'll take the inventory cost for this specific event off at $500. You still only made $80 profit. See how that works. What do you do with the $80 that you profited? Do you treat yourself to an expensive dinner on the last night before you go back home? OR Do you save it or invest it back in your business? I normally invest it back in my business, so I'll be ready for the next event.

I was at an event once and a very experienced vendor told me that as much as I like attending events, I needed to save and have on hand at least $10,000 by October of the previous year so that I would be ready for the vending season the next year. In other words, prepare for the events you want to participate in and if you don't have it saved or readily available, you save for it the next time around.

You've got to have seed to sow in the ground to get a harvest. You can't rely on sales to pay off the credit card debt. It rarely happens. Having cash on hand or in the bank to pay out right or via a debit card for the event is the best way. If you live in the U.S. and have registered your company with your state's Secretary of State, all of this is considered a business expense. Anything surrounding your business travel including vending, food, gas, hotel and other expenses are business expenses. Disclaimer, be sure and check with your tax and business advisor on your specific state rules but in my state, that's the way it's done. Before going to an event, be sure to check what that state's requirements are to sell in that state. In Alabama, I have to get a business license for every city that I sell product. I have a business license for Montgomery, Huntsville, Mobile and Selma.

I make money selling my books and gaining leads at events but I also utilize events as my up close and personal research, find out what the general public likes to read and wants to read, connect with other vendors to possibly collaborate, get ideas on how to be a better vendor/exhibitor, share things that I know with other vendors, ask tons of questions, connect with bookstores, meet with potential clients, check in, check on or meet up with existing clients and then make more sales on my books. I look at an event totally differently than other people do. Because I consult, coach, teach, podcast, publish, speak and write, I am able to have multiple offers and gain multiple streams of income besides just what exists on the table or in the booth. What's on the table or in the booth are my lead generation materials. My books, business cards, Internet radio shows, podcasts, myself are also for potential customers and clients to get to know me, my business and products and services. Remember you are a part of the lead generation as well. Your personality, how you talk to people, your level of understanding about the products and services that you offer as well as how you look and present yourself people connect with as well. People make a decision to work with me based on who they met at the event. I have to be ready to meet people whether I'm tired, hungry, anxious, disappointed or disgusted. I sow seed in the ground of my business to reap a harvest to sow MORE seed into the ground to grow my business.

I've written 100+ books. I usually sell a lot of books at events. At this one event, I had only sold 10 books. Ten books are better than nothing, but I was disappointed to say the least. Because I have so many books, I wait until the very end to leave because I have so much to pack up. I've also learned that there are people who may come late to the event. Fortunately, this day, a lady was running late. I was one of a few vendors still there. Why did she buy 21 books from me?! It doesn't always happen, but it happened that day.

When she walked up, I was disappointed, but she didn't know it. I was a little disgusted at the crowd but she didn't know it. My husband and I smiled and kept putting books in the bag and adding up the credit card receipt.

Sowing and reaping, selling and restocking, is a part of the vicious commerce cycle. If a corn farmer eats all of the corn with no corn to plant, he will have nothing to sow in the spring and nothing to harvest in the fall. It is a law.

I had a new client who ordered books and sold out all of the books which is great. He reached out to me to ask about ways to get funding to get more books to sell. The author spent all of the profits from the book sales. The funding was in his hand, but he used all of the profit for something else. Sure, spend of the profits on you for your hard work but always have some of the profit to put back into the inventory or the business.

By the way, no matter if you call it a side hustle, hobby or "just something I do on the side" it IS a business. Treat it like a business and it will bless you, your family and potentially to the next generation. Take it seriously. Learn all that you can, get better and better at your craft and watch that gift grow and bring you before great men.

Again, don't eat up the seed. Another opportunity will come along, and you won't be ready. You'll have to wait on the next time around but hopefully, you'll be better and reap an even greater harvest than before. NO seed, No harvest.

Notes

Next (Yes, No, One and Done)

This is a phrase about events between my husband and me, "Is this a one and done or will we consider doing this event again next year?" #transparentmoment #getinmyfeelings #stillhuman

I have made a decision regarding returning to events too hastily and quickly before the event even started. I didn't like where my booth was placed on the floor plan only to find out that the floor plan was revised, and I was in the best position at the event. I have made judgments based on how the vendor coordinators talked to me when I entered, and the people nearly bought everything I had and I returned to an event. There have been so many things that have contributed to me emotionally at an event that I now tell myself "do not make a judgment call about an event until it is over." Wait. No matter how much you paid, where your booth or table was located, how much you sold, how many people you met and how many contacts that you made. You canNOT make a clear, decisive judgment on anything regarding an event until you walk out that door. Say that to yourself before entering any event. If you're like me and female, you are emotional. You know how much money, time, effort and energy go into participating in any event. So, when it doesn't look like I'm going to be positioned for success, I get in my feelings. I am just honest about that. But after so many years of this, I have to tell myself, "no judgment until it's over."

Even after the event is over, I have to think about and write down the negatives vs. the positives of an event. At the end of this chapter, use the "Event Recap" document to analyze an event. Be honest. What did you contribute to make the event a success? Did you promote? Did you share? Remember your combined goals for the event. Calculate in what your costs were to attend and then make a judgment as to whether you will participate again next year or ever. Time and life are short. Money is hard to come by and you can make more money, but do you want to spend your hard-earned money at this event? It's your call. You are the business owner. Let's go!

I have written more pages in this book than I intended to when I first started so you can imagine that I have many more stories to tell about being at events. Just let me give these couple of examples. Remember in the previous chapter I talked about the lady who showed up late to the 2-hour event and bought 21 products from me before I left? It was a one and done event until that happened. You just never know. Next year my decision to participate may be the date on the calendar or the other events that I have to attend before or after the event so I can't make a judgment call based on one thing. You have to put the entire event and everything that happened at the event before you can put it in a category of never returning or whether to return or not.

On the other hand, the one and done or not returning to an event sometimes has nothing to do with a negative situation or lack of sales but the season for being there has ended. It's not good or bad, it's just over.

The audience that a particular event has seen what you have to offer, and you haven't produced anything new and until you do, you don't need to go back. They bought from you before, look at your booth/table and realize, I have that. This happened to me when I went to a state event and sold more than 300 products, but when I went to the national event, the people that saw me on the state level stopped by but the events were too close together and I hadn't produced anything new to sell, so they walked off. Now that wasn't the people's problem but my problem of production and opportunity. As you can tell, I travel a lot so for me, these are things to consider.

I mentioned in earlier chapters about non-profit events and/or events that you attend for introduction, exposure and not necessarily for sales. You have to determine what you want from those events and if you are not receiving it, make a decision and stick to it. Exposure with no benefits, movement or results should be very short lived and have a due date on your participation.

There are so many factors to consider when attending events that you have to either have to have a checklist in your mind or one on paper to decide.

Event_____	
Negatives	**Positives**

Return to the Event?
_____Yes _____NO

Event_____	
Negatives	**Positives**

Return to the Event?
_____Yes _____NO

Event_____	
Negatives	**Positives**

Return to the Event?
_____Yes _____NO

Event	
Negatives	Positives

Return to the Event?
_____Yes _____NO

Conclusion

Thank you for purchasing and reading this book. Here are some final things that have come to mind or that I want to reiterate right here.

All pursuits in life, whether success or failure, come with risk. I don't care if it is an educated risk, a heavily researched risk, a no brainer risk a no-risk venture, they are lying: all pursuits especially major pursuits in life are a risk. Yes, do your homework, research, ask questions, find out answers and repeat multiple times but in the end, it will be a yes or a no to the risk. Always weigh the risk vs. your career, business, life and family. It matters. As you get older, it will matter even more and I tell my friends now, "my 'no' game or telling you no is MUCH stronger than saying yes." Why? Because time and life are SHORT. Standing on the outside and looking in, all people have an opinion on how you live your life and what you should have accomplished in your business and life. But listen, all of that comes with a risk of expectation and access. Once you expose yourself, your life, family and business to a high level of media attention, trouble, trials, tribulations and temptations will be knocking at your door. That's a HUGE risk too. Decide wisely and prayerfully.

Be careful about your connections and seek to have the systems in place to make your life, business, surroundings or environment better.

Finally, each event or encounter is a risk. Go into each event, prayerful that God have you meet the people, hear the message and receive the information that you need for your next and your now. You've read the prospectus and event rules. You made the decision to participate. You've paid the entry fee. You've promoted that you're going to be there. You have your inventory; promotional materials and it is on your calendar. Show up to the event for you, your brand and your life. You will make the event better just by your showing up and I guarantee that no matter what happens, how much you sell or who you meet, you will have a story, testimony and life lesson to share for this and the next generation. Let's go!

About the Author

Julia Royston spends her days doing what she loves, writing, publishing, speaking and "Helping You Get Your Message to the Masses, Turn Your Words into Wealth and Be a Book Business Boss." That is her why and motto. Julia is the author of 100+ books, co-authored 10+ books, 15+ sketchbooks and journals, published 400+, recorded 3 music CDs and coached more than 250+ "to be" published authors. She is the owner of five companies, a non-profit organization and the editor of the *Book Business Boss Magazine*.

To stay connected with Julia, visit www.juliaakroyston.com.

Social Media

Facebook — @juliaaroyston

IG — @juliaaroyston

LinkedIn — @juliaaroyston

TikTok — @juliaaroyston

Other Books by This Author